The old-time pamphlet ethos is back, with some of the most challenging work being done today. Prickly Paradigm Press is devoted to giving serious authors free rein to say what's right and what's wrong about their disciplines and about the world, including what's never been said before. The result is intellectuals unbound, writing unconstrained and creative texts about meaningful matters.

"Long live Prickly Paradigm Press.... Long may its flaming pamphlets lift us from our complacency."
—Ian Hacking

Prickly Paradigm is marketed and distributed by The University of Chicago Press.

www.press.uchicago.edu

A list of current and future titles can be found on our website and at the back of this pamphlet.

www.prickly-paradigm.com

Executive Publisher
Marshall Sahlins

Publishers
Peter Sahlins
Ramona Naddaff
Seminary Co-op Bookstore

Editor
Matthew Engelke
info@prickly-paradigm.com

Design and layout by Daniel Murphy.

Presence and Social Obligation

Presence and Social Obligation:
An Essay on the Share

James Ferguson

PRICKLY PARADIGM PRESS
CHICAGO

Prickly Paradigm Press, LLC
5629 South University Avenue
Chicago, IL 60637

www.prickly-paradigm.com

ISBN: 9781734643510
LCCN: 2021930244

Printed in the United States of America on acid-free paper.

Contents

Preface:
On Rethinking the Social
in a Pandemic

This essay is not about COVID-19. It is about social obligation, including the social obligation to share, and where such obligation comes from. It argues that what I call "presence"—the condition of being in physical proximity to others—brings with it a shared vulnerability and a kind of involuntary commonality that undergirds such social obligation.

Contagious disease is a vivid illustration of the link between presence and vulnerability. In the original talk from which this essay emerged, I used a cholera epidemic as an illustration of this link. COVID would serve just as well. But the vulnerability of presence is not, in my view, fundamentally a matter of biology. It is not a matter of "bare life"—a nonsocial, merely biological relation. On the contrary, in my account here, the fact of being alongside another is a fundamentally *social* fact. Nonetheless, perhaps we are learning something about the power of presence as we live through a pandemic that so often deprives us of it.

In recent months, public-health officials have accustomed us to the phrase "social distancing." Some (including many anthropologists) have objected to the usage, observing that the physical distance of concern to epidemiologists is not the same thing as what social scientists mean by "social distance." At my university, a well-meaning administrator wrote to students, correcting public-health usage ("actually, social distance is not the right term: we are talking about physical distance"), while assuring the students that mere physical distance need not endanger the university's warm "community."

But it was not lost on the recipients of this message that the assurance of an uninterrupted warm and intimate experience of community came in the form of a mass e-mail—and that it was followed only hours later by news of the indefinite postponement of the 2020 commencement ceremony. Perhaps spatial distance is not as distinct from social distance as we may have thought. Certainly, the conjuring of social solidarity (or "community") that such a ceremony requires is severely compromised—as Émile Durkheim would have immediately recognized—without the embodied physical presence and sensory experiences that come with it. The patent inadequacy of the online "Zoom celebration" that was offered as a substitute for the commencement only seemed to underline the fact that sociality (and especially the sociality of ritual solidarity) is not fundamentally a matter of transmitting information, but of sharing a distinctive kind of experience.

If welcoming new initiates into a social collective requires a certain kind of presence, so, it seems, does the violent expulsion from the same. Or so I thought in reading a COVID-related story in today's newspaper.[1] The facts of the story are on the face of it perhaps not so extraordinary: the story reports that a convicted drug dealer in Singapore has just been sentenced to death. But the scandal of the story (and what makes it COVID-related) is that the criminal was, in a historic first, sentenced to death *over Zoom*. The shocking thing here—the real moral affront—is neither the drug dealing nor even the execution but the obscenity of sentencing a man to death without looking him in the eye, without sharing a human presence with him.

Social obligation, I argue in this essay, is obligatory. It rests not just on empathy and warm sentiments but on certain vulnerabilities that are linked to physical presence. That shared vulnerability is always with us, in some sense. But there are specific circumstances that sometimes render it especially visible. The COVID pandemic has brought us such circumstances, and may in this way do us the intellectual service of bringing a kind of mournful clarity to things. If so, the least we can do is to try to put that clarity to good use.

1
Introduction:
Why Social Obligation? Why Now?

There is today an urgent need for new thinking about social obligation. I have come to this conclusion through my work over the last decade on what I call the politics of distribution, by which I mean simply the political questions of *who gets what, and why*. In answering such basic questions, we inevitably confront both the issue of sharing (How are the things of value in our world to be divided up among us?) and the problem of obligation (What binding considerations allow or mandate particular distributions, and what makes these considerations in fact binding?). But the ways that we can answer these questions are at present in the midst of quite fundamental changes. In particular, the two main pillars that have supported our thinking about why certain people should or should not receive distributions are increasingly inadequate to the task. These pillars are *labor* and *citizenship*.

Both in my own area of specialization (southern Africa) and across the global South and beyond, the old recipes for authorizing and legitimating distributive claims leave out huge populations. With respect to claims based on labor, growing masses of unemployed and underemployed and the rapid expansion of precarious and so-called "informal" livelihoods increasingly challenge the idea of universal inclusion through integration into a stable, formal-sector workforce (a world of "proper jobs," as I have discussed elsewhere in partnership with Tania Li[2]). Meanwhile the (typically citizenship-based) "social" distributions that have often provided support on grounds other than as a payment for labor (pensions, disability payments, unemployment insurance, "welfare") are increasingly unavailable to many of those who need them most, as an increasingly mobile global population leaves growing numbers, all over the world, undocumented—and thus lacking access to citizenship-based social protection in their places of work and residence.

At the same time, emergent new forms of distributive politics show the importance of different kinds of distributive claims in these times—claims based neither on labor nor on citizenship but on what we might call (in the broadest sense) "ownership," on the one hand, and what I term "presence," on the other. I'll explain these rather cryptic terms shortly. But let me start by reviewing very briefly those old distributive ideals grounded in labor and citizenship, and how they have lately come into question.[3]

With respect to the labor side of the story, all across the world a kind of metanarrative of economic progress has long promised, as a culmination of the "development" process, the universalization of waged or salaried employment—a modern society was supposed to be a society of jobs and jobholders. That this promise has so often been broken does not diminish its attraction, as is clear in the rhetorical appeals of politicians the world over: jobs, jobs, jobs! But a limited ability to think beyond the jobs-for-all promised land afflicts not only politicians but scholars as well. Indeed, the "proper job" has served for so long as a presumed norm or telos of "development" that we are too often left with a stunted and reactive set of categories and concepts for thinking about all the other ways in which people make their way in the world. This is perhaps why discussions of so-called precarity often rely on residual categories of analysis (*un*employment, *in*formal economy, *non*standard employment, *in*stability, *in*security) that render everything outside the world of "jobs" a kind of negative space, defined by that which it is not.

There was a powerful vision implicit in the idea of an emerging "developed" world in which paid labor might provide the basis both of a stable livelihood and of a kind of social membership or incorporation for all. As people left their preindustrial rural agricultural or pastoral livelihoods, in such a conception, they would be fitted into the modern new social order precisely by having "a job"—that enchanted object that still provides the normal answer to the question "So, what do you *do*?" A set of gendered expectations about the breadwinner and the family; the organization of time and space; the role of formal education; respectability and virtue; and contribution to the nation were all rolled into this notion of the "proper job."

Today, as that imagined universality gradually recedes in the rearview mirror, its once-dominant status begins to become visible to us as distinctive, perhaps even strange. As Guy Standing once memorably put it, the twentieth century, in retrospect, now appears as "the century of laboring man," a time when the lifeway of what had been a small fraction of the population (the stabilized urban working class) became, quite suddenly (and somehow—for many—quite convincingly), projected as the future of all.[4] And if "the century of laboring man" is, as Standing argues, at an end, it is not because stable waged and salaried labor is disappearing in any absolute sense, but because it is losing its plausibility as the universal solution, the obvious telos of a worldwide developmental process. Whether due to the globalization of supply chains and labor markets that undercuts established working classes, the persistent structural unemployment and casualization induced by neoliberal restructuring and "austerity," or the recent and looming technological developments that threaten to eliminate or drastically reduce whole categories of paid labor, the old transition story no longer convinces.

One effect of this lost conviction is the apparently worldwide contemporary anxiety about jobs and the social and economic stability they were long expected to anchor. The anxiety springs from a perception that increasing proportions of the population, across much of the world, can no longer rely upon (or even plausibly hope for) the sort of stable waged or salaried labor that has long counted as a "proper job." And this worry is not confined to poor countries, where whole populations appear as "surplus" to the needs of capital (manifest in durably high levels of so-called "structural unemployment"); in rich industrialized countries, too, the loss of manufacturing jobs and general economic insecurity also raise the specter of what Michael Denning has termed "wageless life."[5]

Meanwhile, in the political domain, the nation-state has long provided the same sort of anchor of stability that the "proper job" was supposed to offer in the economic. A legally authorized political membership, in theory at least, underpinned a set of explicit and universal rights and obligations. And this, too, helped provide the answer to those central questions of distributive politics: Who gets what, and why? If income, in "labor" terms, was seen as a reward for work, there always remained the question of all those who did not (in those terms) "work" (i.e., those unable to work, or whose work was not paid). Children, old people, and, often, reproductive women were styled as (in the terminology of the times) legitimate "dependents"— dependent upon the "worker," the "breadwinner," the "head of household." But there were others unable to work, too—due to disability, for instance, or to the unemployment produced by the unpredictable vacillations of the business cycle. And here, the nation-state sometimes took on a directly distributive role, especially in the form of so-called "welfare states" that (where they existed) offered a different kind of legitimate dependence, in the forms of direct social payments to "the poor" and the so-called safety net. Social assistance—perhaps the purest instance of direct state intervention into distributive outcomes—was here explicitly linked to the two "anchors" of distributive politics that I have identified. First, it was generally available *not* to workers but specifically to "dependents" (children, the elderly, the disabled, the reproductive woman)—a kind of photographic negative of the laboring man (the "breadwinner," the "able-bodied worker"). And it was available (again nearly always) only to citizens, as a kind of solidarity appropriately extended only to those within the charmed circle of national membership.

This inflexible coupling of social policy with membership in a nation-state continues to this day, in spite of changing conditions that render it ever more dysfunctional. Meanwhile, visionary programs for redistribution on a global level, such as a planetary universal basic income, fail to gain traction in a world seemingly unable even to conceive of distributive obligation at any level beyond the national.

If the need to rethink the issue of social obligation has lately become urgent, it is because the old ways of authorizing and legitimating distribution that I have described—based on labor and citizenship—no longer work. Instead, such ways leave more and more of the world's population out of the distributive deal altogether, as increasing numbers of people fail to qualify for either the labor frame of inclusion or the national citizenship one. Those falling out of the labor frame include the surging new urban masses who don't gain their livelihoods either from working the land (they are no longer peasants) or by selling their labor (they cannot become workers), but instead pursue what I have elsewhere termed "distributive livelihoods" (i.e., livelihoods that depend not on selling one's labor, but on accessing the income streams of others via social or politics claims).[6] Those falling out of the national frame include those who (with or without access to paid labor) are unable to access citizenship-based forms of distribution (including social protection), often due to migration and the associated lack of documents—the stigmatized so-called illegals who (in southern Africa and elsewhere) make up an increasingly large share of "the poor," but who (as residents but not citizens) lack political rights and distributive entitlements alike. Given these increasingly hard to ignore gaps in the world's systems of distributive allocation, I wish to pose the question of what other grounds (that is, what principles of legitimation and what social and political forces)—beyond those rooted in labor or citizenship—are available to support new sorts of distributive claims? What new ways are emerging for answering the questions "who gets what, and why?" Here, I point to two broad areas of emergence. One I have called "ownership."[7] The other, which I will refer to as "presence," is the subject of the essay that follows this introduction.

With respect to what I am calling "ownership," I begin by observing something that I argued at some length in my book *Give a Man a Fish*, which is that even those who are partly or wholly excluded from the world of productive labor sometimes manage to make strong distributive claims by styling themselves as members of a collectivity understood as a rightful or ultimate sort of "owner." Marxism, with its labor theory of value and its fundamental understanding of the oppressed as "workers" has always struggled with the politics of the nonworker, the so-called "lumpen" masses excluded from the putatively revolutionary class of wage laborers. But I suggested in the book that we are heir to a rich set of alternative Left traditions that may have more to offer to those excluded from a role in the production system. The anarcho-communist Peter Kropotkin, for instance, always insisted on starting with universal claims of distribution and a notion of distributive justice ultimately rooted in societal *membership*, not just labor. Where does our vast wealth come from? Why are we so much more productive than our great-grandparents? We are not better people than they were. We certainly do not work harder. Instead, we are able to produce vast riches they could not have dreamed of, thanks only to an enormous worldwide industrial apparatus of production—an apparatus built up through generations of work, sacrifice, and invention, across centuries, and even millennia, of human history, in a process that generated massive suffering for millions all across the globe. And to whom does this vast wealth-producing apparatus really belong? Surely not only to the corporate stockholders who now (outrageously) claim to own it outright, but to the descendants of all those who worked and imagined and suffered and bled to create it—in short, to all of us. The whole system of production, in this conception, must be regarded as a collective inheritance. And, from this universal claim of common ownership, Kropotkin derives a universal distributive claim: surely, at least some portion of the entire output must be due to each and every one of the rightful owners of the apparatus of production. Everyone, that is, must receive a share.

Note that it is not the worker (as worker) whose claims are prioritized here, but the member of society, the inheritor of a great common estate (in which each and every one of us has a share). It is not just labor that founds that inheritance, in this view, but also things like suffering, bloodshed, ingenuity, and shared experience; it is therefore the entire society that is the source of value. And it is all members of that society (and not only those currently employed as workers) who (as inheritors and co-owners of the whole) are entitled to a rightful share of society's proceeds.

Such arguments, I showed in *Give a Man a Fish*, are not of only academic interest. Indeed, remarkably similar arguments have been put forward by advocates for Namibia's Basic Income Grant campaign, who propose that each and every Namibian should be entitled to a monthly cash payment precisely because they, as the nation's citizens, are the real *owners* of the country and its mineral wealth, and therefore ought to share in the country's wealth.[8] Receipt of a modest monthly state payment, in these arguments, is construed simply as the receipt of a share that is properly due to an owner. The most basic citizenship right is thus understood not as the right to vote, but as the right "to partake in the wealth of the nation."[9] In this conception, direct grants from the state need not bring with them the shame or stigma of receiving charity or getting a "handout"; in receiving a rightful share, Namibian citizens are simply "partaking in the wealth" that rightly belongs to the whole nation. And in doing so, they (as rightful co-owners of that wealth) are not receiving a gift or being offered "help"—they are claiming what is already rightfully their own, a "rightful share."

But such arguments about shares and sharing, however powerful, are founded upon their own form of exclusion, insofar as they are based upon membership in a bounded collectivity (the nation, institutionally represented by the state). And this is linked to the second set of problems I identified at the start: in a highly mobile world, many of the poorest members of many national populations today are those who lack most completely the protections offered by the state, since they are noncitizens. This raises a key question that is both deeply theoretical and inescapably practical: On what basis (*other* than shared national membership) might a distributive obligation (an obligation to share) rest? That is, where rightful shares cannot be claimed on the basis of national membership, what other sorts of grounds might exist for obligatory sharing? To address this question, we must look more closely at the matter of social obligation.

2
Presence and Social Obligation: An Essay on the Share

That obligation must be treated first of all as a specifically *social* matter (and not only, say, a matter of law, ethics, or philosophy) might seem to go without saying for an anthropologist. Certainly, the topic of social obligation has an important and impressive genealogy in the discipline (see "Addendum: Some Theoretical Contrasts and Clarifications"). But it is necessary to observe that "the social" in "social obligation" is not uncontested in these times. It is not only that long-established conceptions of "the social" have been, in recent years, criticized or rethought. Even the very existence of the social is nowadays disputed.

Is the concept of society something we can now simply do without? Nikolas Rose long ago invited us to contemplate what he called "the death of the social."[10] Neoliberal government today, as understood in this Foucauldian frame, operates not on a social body but rather on a network of transacting agents who respond not to obligations but to "incentives." Advocates of actor-network theory, for their part, are happy to reject the concept of "society" altogether, and would have us speak of "the social" only to index a diffuse process of associating things into assemblies (an "activity" that scallops can apparently do as well as people[11]). In the domain of global health, meanwhile, Tobias Rees has reported, in his work on the Gates Foundation, that "the social" is there rapidly vanishing in favor of a new object of knowledge and intervention called "humanity" (which global health practitioners understand as a biologically rather than politically constituted unity).[12]

But without at least some concept of the social, we can hardly invoke something called "social obligation." And I think it is equally true that we miss the true force of the social (and the continuing power of perspectives that rely on the concept) if we fail to identify its deep connection to the idea of obligation. For the "social" in "social obligation" does *not* refer to a biological population, or a network of actants, or a set of economically interested agents linked by markets—it refers (as Durkheim rightly insisted) to a *moral unity*. And for Durkheim, any notion of the social implied precisely "a society"—not just as a collection or association of individuals, but as a certain kind of collective self, with binding obligations on its members. Projects of social criticism and social reform of nearly all stripes have long relied on this conception, in which belonging to a society brings with it certain binding and morally sanctioned obligations.

But what is "a society" today, and what does "social obligation" really mean? We are still haunted by the old, nineteenth-century idea of society as a membership organization, and by the related premise that it is principally the nation-state that defines and bounds a society—a conception that was central both to the birth of the social sciences and to the foundation of "social insurance," "social welfare," and other sorts of (as we say) "social policy." Yet when we confront the great challenges of our time, that old equation of "society" with a collectivity of authorized members of a nation-state fails us spectacularly.

The problem is evident when we deal with noncitizens within our national borders. Here, conceptions of rights and political community rooted in nationality and citizenship confront the harsh reality that many of those most in need of state services and social support are not juridical members of "the society." But the problem is no less obvious when we try to grasp how social obligation applies to those in grievous need in lands that are foreign (but hardly unrelated) to our own (here it is perhaps enough to simply say the word "Syria"). How to think of social obligation in these cases? And what is the relevant "society" that would ground that obligation? Merely national solidarities fail us, while appeals to an imagined "global society" seem to have little force or efficacy. Indeed, we may wishfully invoke abstractions like "global citizenship" and "the world community," but it is clear that these can, under present conditions, sustain only the weakest sort of obligation—that is: the kind that we call "humanitarian."[13]

In *Give a Man a Fish*, I offered an alternative figure of distributive obligation, in the form of the share. A share, I observed, is neither a charitable gift nor a market exchange—its defining feature is that it is based on a common ownership that is prior to all exchange. Sharing therefore entails a kind of social obligation that is rooted neither in reciprocity nor in exchange, but instead in a form of commonality that precedes any act of distribution.[14] It is based not so much on "rights" as on a perception of a rightful state of affairs. In the context of such an understanding, a strong social obligation of one owner to share is simply the obverse of the strong expectation of another *co*-owner to receive his or her *due*—what I called "a rightful share."

But who are the "co-owners" in such an arrangement, and what makes them owners? Where expectations of sharing have been institutionalized at a large scale, in recent decades, it has nearly always been via the principle of membership in a nation-state, and it has been a solidarity at the level of the nation that has undergirded such national institutions as taxation, old-age pensions, and social safety nets. Indeed, even the most ambitious recent proposals for expanding the scope and reach of social protection (such as the proposals for a "basic income" discussed in *Give a Man a Fish*) mostly remain at the level of the nation-state.[15] But if the basis of such sharing is understood as proceeding from membership in a nation (i.e., citizenship in a nation-state), then the closed and exclusionary nature of the membership group presents immediate problems both of principle and of practice. Low-income South Africans, for instance, as members of the nation and owners of its wealth, may well demand "a rightful share" of that wealth—but what about the numerous (and generally even poorer) Mozambicans and Zimbabweans who also live in South Africa? And of course this is hardly a uniquely South African problem. All over the world, increasingly mobile and undocumented populations come together with ever-greater demands on states for service delivery to produce systemic failures of government.

Such observations lead one to wonder if it is really the case that an obligation to share can apply only to a nationally or otherwise bounded membership group? And to ask: What, then, would such a social obligation look like if it were *not* conceived as an obligation toward a pre-given list of "members"? This essay is an attempt to elaborate and explain an idea about how we might answer this question. The idea, proposed in passing in the concluding chapter of *Give a Man a Fish*, was that what I—following Thomas Widlok[16]—called "presence" might serve (along with membership) as a powerful basis for a social obligation to share. Claims rooted in presence (the blunt fact of being "here"), I suggested, may be both more important, and more politically promising, than we have yet realized. If so, attending to the claims of presence (and not just those of membership) might point to new forms of distributive politics that could show us a way out of some of the dead ends into which we have been led by received political frameworks— frameworks that give too much weight to laws, states, and rights, and too little to forms of direct social presence and the social obligations that attach to them. But the suggestion—dropped as it was at the end of a book, and without elaboration or support—was more a provocation than a proper explication. Here, then, I want to develop a formal argument linking presence and the problem of social obligation.

Social Obligation as an Anthropological Problem

My opening move is to treat social obligation not as a philosophical problem, but as an anthropological or even geographical one.[17] Lately, anthropologists have seemed perhaps a bit too quick to flee to the authority of philosophers when it comes time to take on big issues. But I suggest that we might better follow the example of Marcel Mauss here (thus the wildly immodest parallel with his famous *Essai sur le don* implied by the subtitle of this essay). Mauss famously identified three central obligations of the gift: the obligations to give, to receive, and to return. But he did not derive these from philosophical principles, nor did he advocate them as a normative stance. Instead, he described a set of sociological facts—for instance, that the receipt of a gift implies an obligation for a return (an association nicely captured, he noted, in the Polynesian idea of a spirit that resides in the gift, compelling its return). He does not ask why people *should* feel obligation, or even why they do; he takes as his starting place a set of observed facts: across a wide range of cases, people feel that the gift itself impels return. Polynesians have a word for it, but they are not the only ones who feel the force of a set of obligations surrounding gifting. On the contrary, it is simply a sociological fact (in Mauss's account) that the gift is everywhere bound up with these perceived obligations. This, he says, must be our starting place.[18]

In parallel fashion, we might ask: When is the act of sharing a common good *in fact* understood as an obligation? Note that the question is descriptive, not normative. When, that is, would it seem (to the people in question) improper, or even impossible, not to share? Note that such a perception does not mean that such obligations are always met (no more than we would naively suppose that all gifts are in fact reciprocated)—only that it would seem improper or impossible for them not to be. And: Can we identify certain general principles that, across a wide range of ethnographic cases, guide such judgments of an obligation to share (principles like those Mauss identified for the obligations of giving and receiving gifts)?

The obligation to share is often seen as an aspect of scale—characteristic of small groups with "face to face" sociality. But this is neither sufficient (since not all small-scale socialities provoke an obligation to share) nor necessary (since, as I will suggest, there are forms of obligation to share that operate at much higher levels of scale). We can be more precise by specifying the conditions under which we may expect to find an obligation to share. In the most basic possible terms, an obligation to share is normally understood as such when the person whose claim might (or might not) be honored is both:

1. One of us (the attribute of *membership*)
2. Here, among us (the attribute of *presence*)

My claim here is that one of these attributes without the other may have *some* force, but never the *full* force that comes with both membership and presence. The linkage between sharing and *membership* is so familiar to us as to seem banal (whether the division into shares occurs among a small group of friends on the school playground or in the issuance of stock certificates on Wall Street). The link with *presence* is no doubt less familiar. But the importance of presence in establishing claims to shares has been well established in anthropology, and especially in recent anthropological studies of foragers.[19] These studies make clear that allocation of valued goods such as meat, in these societies, proceeds via aggressive demands for shares (so-called "demand sharing"[20]). Demands for shares may rightfully be made by all those present at the occasion of distribution. Shares, in such settings, are not given (out of generosity or benevolence), but *taken* (the share is a "demand," and the "sharing" is compulsory). In the context of such "demand sharing," the answer to the question, "Who is entitled to receive a distribution?" is given by the deceptively simple reply: "Whoever is here." Physical presence is essential—without it, an absent member of a foraging band will have no relevant claim on the meat from a hunt. Shares are distributed only to "those who are here." But of course membership is not without significance either, even among foragers. Just as a member who is not present may lose his or her claims to a share, so even one who is present, if not one of us, may not count as among those who must be attended to. The strongest claims, in general, come from the combination of membership and presence.

Now obviously, to put things so starkly is to ignore all the ethnographic details that would determine, in any particular case, such things as how and under what conditions an obligation to share might be satisfactorily discharged; under what circumstances such an obligation might be refused or ignored; or why some people might receive larger or better shares than others (for there is nothing inherent in the obligation to share that implies either that *all* goods must be shared, or that they must be shared equally). But, as with Mauss's obligations concerning giving, there may be something gained by identifying a very simple set of conditions of obligation that underlie the more complicated concrete forms that socially instituted practices of sharing inevitably take.

In the modern West, we are familiar with the idea that at least some minimal obligations are owed toward fellow members of (as we say) "our own society" (that is, those who are both comembers of the abstract membership set that is the nation, and copresent in the geographical space we call "a country"). Toward those who are in this way both members ("one of us") and present ("here among us"), the fact of a certain kind of social obligation is clear (even if the specific forms it should take are not). Indeed, we sometimes regard these obligations to be of a similar kind, if of less intensity and moral depth, as those owed to members of our families. In contrast to such relatively strong obligation, we may note the weakness both of *presence without membership* (which yields only such fairly feeble forms of obligation toward physically proximate *non*nationals as asylum proceedings) and of *membership without presence*, as when membership in "humanity" (functioning as a kind of analogical extension of the nation) is urgently asserted for distant and foreign others. Such a formulation imposes no real obligation on us—more of an anemic tug of guilt, reproaching us that we really *ought* to feel a vague compassionate concern for distant others who are, after all, still human—and therefore (in this diminished sense) "one of us."

This distinction between criteria of membership and those of presence is, I think, clarifying. But a quick turn to southern Africa reveals how these two principles may be brought together in a more dynamic way than Western political theory often supposes, as presence and membership there often sit in a much more fluid relationship. In European societies, "blood and soil" have long served as principles of exclusion (such that one may be expelled or excluded either for having the wrong descent, or for being born in the wrong place). But southern African societies are (in the *longue durée*, if not always at present) historically disinclined to kick out foreigners, and highly sophisticated at devising means for incorporating them as what is sometimes called "wealth in people." And in the service of securing such wealth, they have traditionally had a more supple and lively conception of how belonging may be linked to both territory (including soil) and bodily substances (including blood). Over time, foreigners have often been held to become durably attached to a place through things like labor (as their sweat mingles with the soil) and suffering (as shared suffering and spilled blood creates a spiritual unity rooted in the lived experience of co-dwelling).[21] Here, it is not juridical citizenship that is at issue (where you were born, who your parents were) but the material entailments of shared physical presence: suffering through the same drought, sweating into the same soil. Being "here," in this long political tradition, counts for a lot—and over time, such physical presence actually *becomes* both a kind of membership and an identity of substance.[22]

A neighbor is therefore a position from which strong claims can emerge. A gifted Zambian ethnographer, Patience Mususa, has recently given a fine example of this from the Copperbelt.[23] Having purchased for her own use a fixer-upper house in an urban neighborhood of Luanshya, Mususa was soon approached by a neighborhood man, who asked if he and his family might move into a spare room at the back of her property, on the understanding that his wife would in exchange serve as a domestic worker. The ethnographer politely declined, and explained that she did not need a domestic worker, and did not intend to rent out the room. But when she took possession of the property a few weeks later, she found that the family had simply moved in. Her outrage was quickly checked, though, by the reactions of her neighbors, who asked just *what*, then, she *did* intend to do with the room. In their eyes, she realized, "to have an unoccupied building would have been too selfish indeed," and she reluctantly let the family stay. In a similar incident, she reported finding one day, upon her return home from work, two strange women helping themselves to some vegetables she had planted in her back garden. Unperturbed, the women cheerfully shouted, "We are just stealing some vegetables from your garden!" Surely, the ethnographer reflected, "living alone, I could not have eaten all the vegetables in the garden." Such "helpings" (as she calls them) were not only common, they were in a real way "deemed acceptable."[24] As Widlok has rightly insisted, among the most important modalities of sharing must be reckoned the practice of (as he puts it) "refraining from interfering with someone who is about to take something."[25] This is the logic of demand sharing, and the rightfulness of the share is here rooted precisely in the simple presence of adjacency, the fact of being "here," the status of being a neighbor.

Yet the power of this social and political logic of presence, I suggest, remains significantly underanalyzed. Even as what I have called the "membership" principle ("one of us") is both explicitly acknowledged in law (as citizenship) and endlessly subject to critical analysis (as the politics of identity), the "presence" principle ("here, among us") has largely remained at the level of common sense. We have not yet fully realized either how central it is to enabling actual obligations, or how richly constructed is the apparently self-evident condition of being present, of being "here."

In the next section, therefore, I turn to the question of what might be gained through the conceptual and political reworking of the idea of presence as the basis for a modern-day politics of sharing.

Scaling the Share

To undertake such a reworking of the relation between sharing and presence requires moving from the sort of literal, face to face presence that we see in the forager band, or in that Copperbelt neighborhood, to a retheorized and expanded concept more suitable to modern distributive politics. This means first of all addressing the problem of scale. An obligation to share is most readily grasped at the microlevel of personal interaction, and we have a harder time imagining how it might apply to larger scales. But why is this? And why do we so easily imagine *membership*, in contrast, as capable of being "scaled up" to hundreds of millions (as in the idea of national citizenship uniting people in a way that is analogous to membership in a family)? What would a similarly "scaled up" conception of "presence" look like?[26]

In fact, the modern politics of state-service delivery reveal at least certain elements of the sort of conception of presence that we need. While we may think of the receipt of services as linked to rights held by citizens, practical imperatives of governance often mean that legal certainties of citizenship and rights give way to other logics entailed in the day-to-day management and administration of populations—an activity that, as Partha Chatterjee long ago pointed out, often involves less the representation of citizens than the government of what he called "denizens."[27] Which children should attend school? Who gets vaccinated for measles? Who gets toilets? The answers often proceed not according to a logic of right, but of practicality.

Do we want undocumented kids *not* to be in school? What, then, would they do, and with what consequences? Do we really want to exclude a huge chunk of the population from our vaccination campaigns? Not legal abstractions but brute sociological and immunological facts give the answers to such questions: certain services must, for practical as much as ethical reasons, be extended not to whoever is an authorized member, but to whoever is here.

As Anne-Maria Makhulu has shown for South Africa, direct action by people lacking legal rights (such as squatters building houses illegally) has often amounted to an extremely effective political strategy (both in the apartheid period and much more recently).[28] More broadly, service delivery demands of all kinds (for housing, for electricity, for water, for road maintenance) have generally been the most effective form of popular politics in South Africa in recent years. This has involved medical services as well as infrastructure struggles around things like sanitation and water. South Africa has become famous for a fierce and theatrical politics of toilets, for instance, while battles over household water delivery are resolved through grudging acknowledgments that even illegal settlers who are, in official logics, "not supposed to exist" will die without water, even as contagious diseases follow their own laws, stubbornly refusing to distinguish between a South African and a Mozambican. All these forms of political assertion and pragmatic accommodation have drawn their force less from the claims of citizenship than from those of presence; the problems of government that they have presented have involved less adjudicating the rights belonging to members than coping with the material demands of what we might term *adjacency*.

An idealized democratic town-hall meeting often provides a kind of stylized image of the essence of political *membership*—an intimate sociality that we imaginatively scale up to the level of the nation-state as a picture or model of a participatory political community. In a similar spirit, let me offer a contrasting image for the essence of *presence*: the African minibus taxi. These local taxis are known by various names across the continent (*makombi, matatu, dala dala, tro tro*), but they have an instantly recognizable set of features. Typically, they are overloaded, with passengers stuffed in like olives in a jar, pressed up against each other. They are hot, sweaty, uncomfortable, and sometimes dangerous. But they are also sites of a kind of shared sociality, where certain minimal standards of good manners and civil conduct are generally well respected. I offer this as an image of sociality understood as a kind of accidental copresence (as opposed to a community of membership founded on a shared identity).[29] The taxi experience involves a sociality rooted in involuntary and haphazard association. Linked neither by a unity of social kind or shared substance (like a family) nor one of shared interest or affiliation (like a club), the passengers have only an incidental and contingent relation to each other. They are merely adjacent. But this adjacency imposes a nontrivial sociality that entails real obligations and a more or less continuous set of pragmatic adjustments. Each time new passengers board, the old ones must rearrange themselves, give way, yield a precious share of that scarce, tightly packed space. There is no social contract here, not even any real reciprocity. It is something more like demand sharing. When new passengers enter the vehicle, we are obliged: we feel we *must* give up at least some space, must make ourselves less comfortable, simply because someone else (with the same needs as we have) has appeared.

Let me be clear that I offer this image only as an aid to the imagination, and not as an analytic. That is, I propose using the figure of the taxi in just the same way that those seeking to render the idea of a national "political community" plausible might use the idealized image of the town-hall meeting: as an imaginative device for linking scales. We do not suppose the town-hall image is an accurate model of how American society "really works," or that real town-hall meetings are somehow spaces of pure and uncoerced democratic decision-making. What the "town hall" figuration offers is not an analytical model of a political system but a way of imaginatively linking the abstractions of large-scale political membership with a set of practices at a more readily graspable scale. I offer the image of the taxi and its shared space in the same spirit—it is not meant as some sort of microcosm or naive sociological model but as a way of providing "presence" with some of the same sort of imaginative immediacy that nation-state "member-ship" has so long enjoyed via countless metaphors of nation-as-family, nation-as-community, and (as in the town-hall example) nation-as-small-town.

This image may help us contrast my approach to sharing as obligation with the "humanitarian reason" described by Didier Fassin.[30] Humanitarian action, in this account, involves a mode of ethical contemplation through which feelings of empathy and compassion for strangers move us to generosity. Encountering a true *obligation*, though, is not a matter of compassion, and may as likely provoke annoyance or anger. Indeed, irritation rather than pity is often the sign of real obligation: like when your no-good brother fails to pay his rent because he spent all his money on drugs, and now wants to sleep on your couch and probably throw up on it like he did last time, and for sure will mess up your apartment for God knows how long—and what do you say? Probably not: "Oh, I feel so sorry for him that I am moved to generosity!" but something more like: "How incredibly annoying—but what can I do, he's my brother?!" *That* is what real obligation feels like. Indeed, as the geographers Clive Barnett and David Land have observed, when we make actual allocative decisions, it is normally *not* as isolated, contemplative Kantian subjects, but in real social contexts, where thinking about sharing unfolds in the push and shove of active social relationships and active claims and demands.[31] And it is these relationships and these active claims and expectations (more than abstract ethical reasoning) that actually drive allocative outcomes (often leaving us feeling, as in the case of the no-good brother, as if we had no real choice). Like giving way in the crowded minibus, we are not simply acting out of a discretionary and beneficent generosity. We are under real obligation. Obligations are obligatory.[32]

Note, too, that while I've invoked biological contagion as one sort of issue of adjacency, the relation of presence is fundamentally a *social* rather than a biological relation. This is not a matter of the "bare life" that Agamben linked to the image of the camp: a zone of merely animal life socially separate from us.[33] Rather, the most elementary sort of *social* relation is at issue—like in the minibus, we are dealing with the other who presses up against you, and therefore must be dealt with. It is a matter not of "humanity," but of the person next to you. As the inimitable G. K. Chesterton expressed it:

> "We make our friends; we make our enemies; but God makes our next-door neighbour. Hence he comes to us clad in all the careless terrors of nature; he is as strange as the stars, as reckless and indifferent as the rain. ... That is why the old religions and the old scriptural language showed so sharp a wisdom when they spoke, not of one's duty toward humanity, but one's duty toward one's neighbour."[34]

Just as the supposition that the only alternative to the market is the gift has blinded us to other distributive principles (like the share), so may the presumption that the only alternative to the exclusions of national or societal membership is a universalist or cosmopolitan humanism have blinded us to other possible figurations of social obligation.

Demands for service delivery (of the kind, as I've noted, that are made by "denizens" as readily as citizens) are in fact a "scaling up" of precisely the sorts of demands that proceed from these relations of neighborly "pressing up against"—of what I have called adjacency. Because we're *here*, say new urbanites across the great metropolitan centers of the global South, we must have toilets. We must have clean water. Our children must go to school. We must, in some minimal sense, be attended to—even served. And, in some grudging way, they usually are.

Now let me be clear: such acknowledgments of the claims of presence are often absolutely minimal, and in no way satisfactory. They are generally conceded only with the greatest reluctance, and they normally come with explicit limitations and undisguised inequalities in relation to the claims of full membership that are available to citizens. But it is also true that such concessions to presence, in the domain of service delivery and elsewhere, do lead to real, if unequal, distributions of resources. They result, that is, in a real yielding of shares. Just as you really must make room in the crowded minibus, even if you are cursing under your breath, so even the most reluctant citizens must pay the taxes that enable poor migrant children to go to school (even as they may at the same time deny migrants' political rights and even denounce their very existence).

Glimpses of such an emergent politics can be seen in some recent anthropological work on infrastructure and urban environments in Africa. Here, we find political problem-spaces of government within which urban residents are drawn together not just as fellow citizens—linked by language, culture, or abstract membership in a nation—but as co-users of an urban infrastructure. Antina von Schnitzler's ethnography of urban water distribution in South Africa, for instance, traces a politics in which services are obtained via administrative links to the state, and accessing a vital good like water involves not only a democratic politics but also a range of material demands, illegal acts (illegal connections, nonpayment) and advanced technologies (prepaid water meters).[35] Ideas of citizenship and rights are mingled in amid these struggles for administrative recognition, to be sure. But it is less legal abstractions that are at stake here than the material connections through which actual "shares" are obtained. The specifics of service allocation (here, how people get water, how much they get, and how much of that they must pay for) are never simply derived from political or legal principles, but always worked out in the practice of the administrative state. When people succeed in getting water, then, it is never simply as rights-holding citizens, but also as what Chatterjee called "the governed"—populations who figure as an administrative problem to be solved, via a process that is not only political, but also material and technical.[36]

The stage for the struggles over water that von Schnitzler analyzes was set by a revealing prior episode in which the South African state first committed itself to a form of universal provision to all residents (not only citizens) of a basic minimum of free water. This guaranteed quantum of so-called "lifeline" water is now a firmly established fixture of South Africa's water politics, but it was not part of the newly independent state's original plans for water provision, which largely focused on "cost recovery." With this goal in mind, the policy was to attempt to collect "user fees" from all legitimate recipients of water, and to simply cut off service to those who were "not supposed to have it"—including noncitizens and those who would not or could not pay. But this strategy came crashing down once its consequences became clear, in the form of a cholera epidemic in KwaZulu-Natal in 2000–2001. Those who were cut off from the municipal water system, unsurprisingly, had improvised their own solutions, drawing water from nearby fetid ditches and pools. And before long it became clear that cholera was not interested in who did or did not "deserve" to get it, as bill-paying South Africans were soon taken down by the same germs that infected the foreign migrants and the nonpaying indigent. Again, claims to services here were granted—to the (always limited) extent that they were—not as a matter of the rights of citizens but of the inescapable pragmatics of presence.

In another recent example, Jacob Doherty's work in Kampala shows us a different urban scene, one in which people are most powerfully linked less by political integration (as citizens) or by economic integration (in a system of production) than via a kind of urban ecology of waste and disposability.[37] Struggles over waste unfold in a context where both conventional electoral politics and labor-based mobilizations play a part, to be sure. But along with such familiar elements of African urban politics, Doherty foregrounds a set of distributive struggles that are not reducible to them. These involve the distribution of things that directly follow from physical copresence—the distribution of medical risk; the distribution of the social stigma of waste and odor; the distribution of mobility (with its pleasures and dangers) across an overcrowded and contested landscape of urban transit. Low-income people are themselves often rendered a kind of waste in this cruel politics—suffering a socially constructed disposability, even as they (like some of Kampala's animal life) sometimes find niches within they can not only survive but even attain a kind of tainted flourishing amid the filth. Here, the question of the distribution of life's goods (and "bads") is decided through a visceral and intimate embodied politics of value and stigma, status and stench.

Gabrielle Hecht, meanwhile, offers an account of the political landscape left in the aftermath of the vast South African mining industry—an industry whose slow but steady decline has left behind a toxic archipelago of dumps and mine tailings that disrupt and endanger urban life across much of the country (and especially the densely populated Rand).[38] Scholars of the region know, of course, that the old production apparatus of mining generated a range of powerful social identities and forms of political leverage. What we are now starting to see is that its toxic aftermath is generating very different political issues, raising issues less of labor control and class formation, and more of co-use, proximity, and shared environmental vulnerability. After all, you don't have to be a mineworker to be affected by mining's toxic aftermath, and the map of vulnerability that this toxicity has created does not align well with the more familiar mappings of labor or of citizenship. This means that even as we register the decline of a powerful and familiar form of Left politics centered on working-class mobilization, we must simultaneously face the challenge of analyzing the new configurations of political dangers and possibilities that are emerging in the aftermath of that decline. Here, as in the other brief examples I have given, the witnesses to the death of one kind of politics must interrupt their mourning to attend to the birth of another.

In all the cases that I have mentioned, concrete questions of who gets what are worked out through embodied and spatialized practices enacted by people who have been thrown together into physical proximity, into a kind of shared copresence. And these people typically engage in these practices not as authorized members of a preconstituted social body (a nation or a polity) but as participants in unintentional and often involuntary sorts of collectivity. Politics, under these conditions, I have suggested, is less about abstract political membership and more about de facto co-usage and the pragmatic accommodations of copresence.

This is not, of course, to say that nations, citizenship, and legal rights somehow don't matter anymore, only that there is an emerging new vantage from which they may have less of a monopoly on the field of politics. The shift in perspective that I have so briefly tried here to evoke, that is, is not a matter of throwing out wrong ideas and replacing them with right ones. It is rather a matter of developing new concepts and lines of sight that bring new objects and processes into view—a shift marked by the appearance of alternative analytical terms such as *presence*, *adjacency*, *accommodation*, *co-users*, and so on.

Such a perspectival shift gives us a way of understanding the politics that often enable the expanding urban populations of the global South to make real and effective (if modest) distributive claims. The new "cities of slums" that have sprung up across the global South in recent decades (often through unauthorized and autoconstructed housing) have been fodder for a catastrophist imagination on both the political left and right.[39] But today, looking back on the dire pictures sketched in these and other turn-of-the-millennium tracts, it is clear that their prophecies of urban doom have mostly not been borne out. To be sure, the lives of urban migrants in the "slums" in question have often involved extraordinary hardship. But most of the time, the "informal" settling of urban peripheries has been experienced by the new urban pioneers themselves not as some sort of disaster, but as a process of gradual and hard-won improvement in their situations.[40] And a significant part of this modest improvement has come about via the access such new urbanites have been able to obtain to infrastructural and other public goods and state services—a kind of "share" (in my terms) that can be claimed only via urban presence. Some of this access can be obtained just by "being there." Roads, lighting, public order, opportunities for scavenging—these are in some measure available for the use of whoever occupies the space. Other goods are sometimes available on an illegal but sometimes de facto tolerated "self-help" basis (e.g., through the diversion of flows of water and electricity). Urban presence may be a condition of possibility, too, for the receipt of certain kinds of patronage, even as actual or implied threats posed by urban masses to elite security or urban space can sometimes provide a kind of leverage for making distributive claims from below.[41]

To be sure, the "shares" thus obtained are by no means equal ones. But as I have noted, there is nothing about sharing that implies shares must be equal. The point is not that the kind of urban presence I have evoked here produces equality, but that it produces a situation within which *some* yielding of shares normally occurs. That is not nothing. Indeed, it may be the difference between life and death for some. But the "sharing" that I identify is not at all some sort of utopian ideal to be celebrated. Rather, the sharing that is enabled by presence is fiercely contested—indeed fought for, tooth and nail—and often granted only grudgingly and under duress. If there is sharing here, it is "demand sharing" all the way through, as (often pathetically small) "shares" are not generously given, out of a magnanimous generosity, but brusquely *taken* by those whose presence gives them the opportunity to do so. In analyzing such decidedly nonutopian political processes, my approach has been to track real developments on the ground, not to propose some imaginary pie in the sky of universal sharing and happily-ever-after.

At the same time, however, I feel that it would be a missed opportunity for a scholar tracing an emergent politics to remain satisfied only to describe what is. After all, one of the main reasons for working toward an understanding of emergent social and political forms is to help us see what might come next, and to enhance our imaginative capacities to conceive of possible future pathways. In that spirit, the final section of the essay moves into a more speculative mode, to consider how a politics of presence-based sharing might, via such pathways, be pushed toward an expanded, even global, horizon of inclusion.

Toward a Global Politics of Presence

The significant distributive results achieved in recent years by claims rooted in presence may perhaps suggest a starting point for a larger political strategy that would work toward more inclusive and universalistic understandings of presence. Perhaps, that is, a more robust and well-thought-out understanding of how being "here among us" leads to social obligations might enable the development of a politics aimed at expanding those obligations and broadening their reach.

If this seems implausible, consider the way that similarly unsatisfactory and unequal constructions of membership provided starting points for more universalistic and progressive constructions of "us," as modern universalistic national citizenship gradually replaced more restrictive conceptions (such as that women were citizens but not voters, or that a black American counted as three-fifths of a human being). Perhaps our understandings of presence (being "here among us") stand ready for a similarly radical inclusionary expansion.

If so, what might emerge is a two-dimensional politics, where one dimension is very familiar to us, and the other much less so, and thus in need of more development and emphasis. The first, familiar dimension involves continuing to work the axis of membership, aiming to extend the sense of "us" via a politics of expanded memberships and solidarities. The second, less familiar one, would involve working to expand the sense of "here" and "among us"—thus strengthening the political claims of presence.[42] Recent work on so-called "geographies of generosity" has discussed the ethical problem of the distant stranger, and the political challenge of finding ways of inducing citizens of affluent Northern societies to develop a stronger sense of responsibility toward anonymous others in distant but impoverished climes.[43] But instead of asking how we can inculcate a strong sense of responsibility toward others who are not present (which I have suggested never seems to work very well), perhaps we might do better to ask how those others can in fact be rendered present.[44]

What might this second strategy look like? We must start with the observation that presence is never a simple physical fact, but rather always depends on elaborate commonsensical constructions that allow some people and things to count as "here" and others (though equally or even more proximate) as not. As a BBC piece on borders recently asked: Why should UK citizens living in Dover "owe more to the inhabitants of Middlesbrough, in North England, 260 miles away, than to refugees in a Calais camp just 26 miles away?"[45] And if some who are very near indeed to us are in this way deemed to lack presence by virtue of being on the wrong side of an imaginary line, it is also true that even being on the right side of the line has often not sufficed to allow a foreigner to count as "here" and "among us." A kind of social invisibility, as ethnographers of the abject have long documented, often makes it possible for us to fail to recognize the presence even of people who are right in front of us. Presence, that is, is neither literal nor self-evident—it must be acknowledged as such, through a political and social process of recognition.[46]

Of course this could happen, in theory, by states simply allowing presence itself to establish legal rights—perhaps even including the full package of

rights associated with citizenship itself (thereby trans-
forming citizenship from a membership-based status to
one based on presence or proximity). This is the thrust
of some recent normative political philosophy.[47] But
this "solves" the problem only at a theoretical level,
and has limited purchase on how presence, in the actual
here and now, is linked to currently existing forms of
recognition that support social obligations.

The more anthropological way forward is to ask
how such recognition of the claims of presence occurs
in actual social practice, and then to seek political strategies that might build on that foundation. How do those
who lack state recognition nonetheless sometimes come
into view as being present and therefore having a claim
to a share? One effective strategy for framing the issue
has often been to focus on economic interdependencies,
and especially on how the products that we all consume
link us to others—others who may be invisible to us,
but whose labor is the condition of our own existence
or prosperity. In this spirit, when I teach an introduction to anthropology course for undergraduates, I use
Seth Holmes's book about the social and human costs
of migrant labor in US agriculture to force students to
think about migrant farm laborers who are in fact not
"members" of our US political society (conceived as
a nation of legal citizens), but who *are* (if sometimes
invisibly) "here among us."[48] Holmes's chief technique
for making them visible as "here among us"—rendering
them "present," in my terms—is to again and again
point to the connections between their labor and our
dependence on the concrete products of that labor.
That crisp green salad you ate for lunch was picked
by someone we must attend to—someone who is here

among us. I do the same thing in my teaching about Africa, when I invite students to contemplate the harsh labor of Zambian mineworkers as it is manifested right before them, in the copper wires that illuminate their classrooms. In spite of great geographical distance, I render the mineworkers present in the same way that Holmes does for the farmworkers who are only an hour away.

Barbara Ehrenreich has made a similar sort of argument: we owe a social obligation, she says—what she styles a kind of gratitude—to many who lie beyond our visible social circles.[49] When we sit down to a meal, we should ask ourselves about (as she puts it) the "whole communities of people," "many of them with aching backs," who made it possible. "Who picked the lettuce in the fields, processed the standing rib roast, drove these products to the stores, stacked them on the supermarket shelves and, of course, prepared them and brought them to the table?"

Such critical strategies do enable us to argue from a kind of presence (even where the political and cultural membership of national citizenship is absent). But as a foundation for social obligation, labor (as I emphasized in *Give a Man a Fish*) may let us down as completely as the nation form does, in these times of mass structural unemployment. Let us imagine, for instance, that the sore-backed workers whom Ehrenreich describes were suddenly replaced by lettuce-picking robots (something that is not difficult to imagine these days). Would my social obligations to them disappear when they move from working poor to unemployed poor? When my lettuce no longer passes through their hands, should I no longer think of them? I don't think so—and I don't think she thinks so. I think she's doing what I do in my class—using the very material connection via labor as a convenient club to beat the reader into recognizing that social obligation exists. But surely our obligation to those who live among us is not really limited only to those who perform services for us—else we would be obliged only to the healthy and able-bodied members of poor communities, but not to the sick and disabled. The division of labor here is a convenient example of social mutuality, but not its source or foundation. And if that is the case, then social obligation is not really a kind of fee paid in reciprocity for services rendered, but something else entirely—not the contractual "I owe you x because you have given me y," but something more like the foragers' "Of course you will join in the meal, because you are hungry and you are here!"

In fact, participation in the production process is seemingly becoming a weaker and weaker sort of ground for making distributive claims, as the labor migrant is increasingly replaced by the refugee, the asylum seeker, the migrant whose labor is expressly *not* needed, and who must try to achieve recognition in other ways. Instead, then, we will need to turn to other features of presence that are much less developed in our critical practice. These features include such things as shared need, to be sure—need that is as evident in the demand for social and medical services in modern contexts of immigration as it is in the collective hunger of the foraging band. But these features also include all forms of shared vulnerability and suffering, and most generally, all the shared problems and possibilities of involuntary copresence.[50]

Conclusion

By way of conclusion, let me briefly pose the question: Where might such an enhanced and expanded politics of presence lead? In the most hopeful case, I would like to think, it might lead all of us, through more or less direct paths, to a stronger and more robust sense of social obligation, one that might be able to break out of the conventional nation-state frame that has for so long colonized our understandings of sociality and obligation alike. If so, such a shift might in a small way help open the door to political outcomes that now seem out of reach—perhaps even including the development of institutions of global redistribution (such as the planetary universal basic income that I mentioned in the introduction).

Even if this is, in the end, too optimistic—that is, even if the direct political payoffs of such an intellectual project are more meager or far off than I have perhaps made them sound—I do think there is important intellectual work waiting to be done on this issue. In recent decades, we have spent a lot of critical and political energy rethinking who counts as "us." We have recognized that taken-for-granted social identities are in fact elaborate and consequential constructions, whose reworking must be at the heart of our politics. We now need an equal dedication to the problem of what counts as "here"—recognizing that commonsense notions of presence (the idea that some people are "here, among us" while others are not) are also elaborate constructions. They, too, require a reworking that ought to be central both to contemporary politics and to engaged intellectual life.

And in the long run, perhaps it is not too much to hope that such an endeavor just might help us find ways of reckoning transnational social obligation that would go beyond such bland and powerless assertions of common identity as "humanity," and help us to arrive at a more robust sense of a real lived commonality. Armed with such a sense, we might start to build a world within which, for all of us—as for foragers sitting down to a shared meal—"being there" might be enough. In such a world, indeed, we might begin to be able to appreciate the full richness of that state of involuntary mutual being that Hannah Arendt called "plurality," which she once characterized as "the joy of inhabiting together with others a world whose reality is guaranteed for each by the presence of all."[51]

3
Addendum:
Some Theoretical Contrasts
and Clarifications

In the interest of readability (and in the Prickly
Paradigm style), the presentation of the arguments in
the previous sections has been light on references. But
more theoretically minded readers may wonder how
my arguments relate to some of the key concepts and
frameworks to which they are (or may seem to be)
related, and it is with that in mind that I offer this short
collection of elaborations and clarifications as a set of
reading notes or extended footnotes. Some of these
notes involve clear and fairly obvious lines of theoretical descent (e.g., my perspective's relation to the
social-anthropology tradition) that I think are worth
elaborating and making more explicit. Others involve
what might seem to be points of theoretical connection
(e.g., Derrida's critique of "presence") that are in fact
more apparent than real (like "false friends" in translation work). Here the point of the note is not to explore

a theoretical engagement so much as to head off a possible misunderstanding. I begin with a discussion of the importance of the social-anthropology tradition for thinking about obligation before proceeding to briefly touch on real or apparent links with the perspectives of a few well-known theorists.

The Social-Anthropology Tradition and the Analysis of Generosity

In the anthropological literature, it is a commonplace to observe that people do not make their way in social life simply doing whatever they please. Social action is always constrained, hemmed in in various ways by a host of social obligations, including obligations to share with, or to be generous toward, others. And a key insight of this literature is that people honor such social obligations not simply out of generous temperaments and warm feelings, but because it would be socially costly for them not to do so. Sometimes this involves a simple fear of punishment or other social sanction applied in response to the breaking of a norm. More often, though, it involves more subtle considerations of social reputation and esteem. Indeed, this is perhaps the most well-known finding in the anthropology of giving (already firmly established in Bronislaw Malinowski's treatment of the Trobriand *kula* and Mauss's analysis of the Kwakiutl potlatch): generosity often comes not from selflessness but from ambition. Generosity, in this perspective, is therefore poorly understood as simply the product of ethical reasoning (I must do *x* because it is right), as such motives are always mingled with considerations of social consequences and reputational gain and loss.

This classically anthropological perspective informs the analysis of what I called "real obligation" in the discussion (see pp. 26–27) of the no-good brother who comes to stay. As I noted, allowing him to stay does not feel like an act of generosity but like something being imposed against one's will—"I have no choice," you say. "What can I do? He's my brother." But why do you feel that you have no choice? Is it that your sense of ethical propriety would prevent you from failing to help your brother? Perhaps. But perhaps you are also thinking about what would happen next if you threw him out. What would be the consequences when he tells your parents about how you have treated him? What about that old friend of his who now has a job at your work-place—what will he will say about you, and to whom? A more ethnographic understanding may reveal that what is involved in this sort of obligation is not just following an abstract ethical rule but trying to find a way (to put it in contemporary terms) not to look like an asshole. The anthropological perspective suggests that, whether we are talking about the *kula* ring in the Trobriand Islands or the houseguest in your apartment, we should be careful not to ignore the ways that expectations about sharing involve genuine obligations enforced by real social consequences and not just sentiments.

Consider the difference between two different dictionary definitions of the word "obligatory." The first definition is *Merriam-Webster*'s primary definition: the obligatory, it says, is something that is "binding in law or conscience."[52] This contrasts instructively with a different definition, provided by Vocabulary.com, which offers as its primary definition that the obligatory is "required by obligation or compulsion or convention."[53] Vocabulary.com goes on to elaborate helpfully: "obligatory describes something you do because you have to, not because you want to."

It is useful to pause a moment over the (for my purposes here, enormous) difference between these two definitions. On my account, the "have to" in social obligation does not come from either ethical contemplation or legal sanction. Instead, it derives specifically from the force of the social—that is, it is linked to what *other people* will think of you, and how *other people* will behave toward you.

I will now try to show how different this specifically social understanding of obligation is from one that departs from the "law or conscience" conception on view in the first definition. Let us consider the well-studied case of the sharing of food, probably the most discussed instance of sharing in the anthropological literature. Such acts of sharing, the anthropological literature shows, come not only from kind feelings or even expectations of reciprocity (though both of these may well be present). They also generally depend crucially on fear of the consequences of *not* sharing. This idea is best illustrated in the "demand sharing" literature on foragers, which clearly reveals that what we call "giving" is often not really voluntary at all, but a matter of submitting to claims that in a real sense cannot be refused. But I emphasize that the underlying dynamic is not unique to foragers, and is well attested in ethnographies of village life across the world.

A characteristic example comes from Elizabeth Colson's work on the agriculturalist Gwembe Tonga people of Zambia. The ethnographer witnessed a local woman's response to a visit from another woman (not especially well known to her) from a neighboring village. When the visiting woman asked for grain, her host unhesitatingly responded by offering her a meal, and filling her grain basket to overflowing. It was an act apparently made out of a gracious generosity, "in the best traditions of Tonga hospitality"—and perhaps also, the ethnographer initially concluded, an instance of what anthropologists of the day called "generalized reciprocity." Only later did the woman who had given the grain reveal another motive, when she offered advice to another village resident on the danger of denying food to those who ask. Who knows, she said, what kinds of medicine people might have, or who might be a sorcerer? "It is not safe to deny them. You saw me give grain to that woman who came the other day. How could I refuse when she asked me for grain? Perhaps she would do nothing, but I could not tell. The only thing to do is to give."[54] Here, as we find so often when we are dealing with real sharing, the decision to "give" is experienced as something over which "the giver" has no real choice.[55]

Vernacular norms and practices of this kind do yield a substantive and significant kind of sharing, offering real (if limited) protection against hunger even to the poorest of neighbors. But such yielding of shares is done not simply out of generosity or empathy, as is so often implied in Western understandings of "giving to the poor." Real obligation, even compulsion, is often involved, and fear may be a prominent motive. As Colson put it, "Anthropologists have a liking for paradoxes, and it should therefore be no surprise to us if some people live in what appears to be a Rousseauian paradise because they take a Hobbesian view of their situation: they walk softly because they believe it necessary not to offend others whom they regard as dangerous."[56]

It is not as if all this has nothing to do with ethical thinking, of course. Social compulsions are normally bound up in complex ways with ethical commitments, and the pressure to give food (in Colson's example) is surely not unconnected to the powerful local ethical principle that it is wrong for some people to go hungry while others have more food than they need. But the point is that it is not *only* ethics that are involved in decisions to share—indeed, I may give you food not because of any sort of ethical judgment at all (neither my own nor my neighbors'), but simply because I fear the consequences if I don't. In a world of proximate sociality (as every ethnographer of village life knows), it can be very costly to have enemies.

This classical anthropological perspective, of course, comes from studies of face-to-face sociality, often at a small scale, and this presents some obstacles to simply generalizing such a perspective to larger scales, as I have discussed (see the section "Scaling the Share," in part 2). But it also offers an important insight that is central to my argument—namely that the power of presence is based on the mutual vulnerability that accompanies it. If adjacency renders others potentially dangerous to me, then I must take some care to attend to the expectations and demands of those adjacent others.

The classical perspective of social anthropology helps us to understand the "social" part of "social obligation," thereby enabling us to understand how a responsibility to share in fact becomes not just a pious ideal, but an actual obligation—an obligation that is obligatory not only in theory but in fact.

Durkheim

Émile Durkheim is a key ancestor in the social-anthropology tradition to which I have just referred, associated particularly with the insistence (which, I have argued, retains its importance today) that social obligations need to be understood as simultaneously moral and social. But Durkheim went beyond this to argue that—especially in societies featuring what he termed "mechanical solidarity"—social norms are not just enforced and legitimated, but sanctified. And on this point he developed an argument about the power of bodily presence that has both a certain affinity with my own position, and a major difference.

Durkheim's intuition (in his analysis of Australian ritual[57]) that the social claims we make on each other are strengthened via bodily presence prefigures my argument in important ways. But the "power of presence" is conceived very differently. My "presence" is not the charismatic and magical crowd of nineteenth-century social-psychological theory, on which Durkheim relied so heavily. It is rather the mundane bumping up against each other of adjacency, the muddling-through of the strangers on the minibus. Obligations, in my account, flow from pragmatic circumstance and shared vulnerabilities, not intimation of the transcendent.

But if I depart from Durkheim's rather mystical ideas of social energetics, I insist on the continuing importance of a concept of the social, and see no analytical advantage in Bruno Latour's attempt to redefine it out of existence.[58] Latour's argument is that we simply have no need to invoke "society" at all. In its place he offers a notion of a process of "association" that links humans both with one another and with other, nonhuman "actants"—but in the process strips such associations of all the key characteristics that, in my account, give social obligation its force. What is lost when "society" is reduced to "association" is precisely the understanding that acting socially means acting in a way that takes account of the obligations you have toward others— and of assessing what those others think of you and your conduct, and how they are subsequently likely to behave toward you. My position does not seek to restore the old organismic "society" of Durkheimian functionalist sociology, but it does reject Latour's facile pseudo-solution to the challenge of rethinking things like social obligation (which seems to be simply to pretend it does not exist, or to declare that it is a false problem). It is often noted that Latour's analyses seem strangely devoid of considerations of morality. Less often noted, but more important for my purposes here, is that they also offer very limited resources for dealing with the issue of social obligation. In the famous case that Latour often uses as an exemplar for the actor-network approach, the scallops (as "nonhuman actants") may be "associated" with us, but they do not worry about what we're thinking about them—nor do they experience real obligation of either the moral or the social sort.[59]

Derrida

Another point of both real connection and possible misunderstanding involves Jacques Derrida's well-known writings on "presence."[60] A theme running through much of Derrida's work is a critique of what he called "the metaphysics of presence," and an extended polemic against the possibility of an unmediated or foundational reality that would be simply "there." Instead, he insisted, objects of knowledge or perception, including the subject itself, are made possible only through a play of difference in which there are no foundations, and everything (including the "systems" of meaning beloved by structuralists) is vulnerable to destabilization via deconstructive analysis.

But the apparent opposition here between Derrida's position (he is "against" presence) and mine (I am "for" it) is only a superficial and misleading one. "Presence" in my account is not any sort of foundation or essence but precisely something that has to be represented and recognized. (As Matthew Engelke has noted, the same is true of ideas of God in Christian theology: God becomes "present" only via a whole set of practices and signs through which that presence is "rendered.")[61] Presence in my sense (being "here among us") is neither a self-evident fact, nor some sort of mystification. Rather, being "here" always involves being *rendered* present. And that requires a representational process, a semiotics (as well as—in my account—a politics). So in my usage, "presence" never plays the role that it does in the views that Derrida attacked: the thing that's simply "there" and therefore requires no deconstruction. On the contrary, I argue just the opposite: that being "here among us" requires the same complex semiotic and political process of construction as being "one of us"; presence is not a foundation, but indeed an endlessly "deconstructable" and reconstructable convention. So what may appear on the surface to be a disagreement with Derrida is at a deeper level an agreement (even if the word "presence" is used differently).

Chatterjee

Partha Chatterjee's work is a significant inspiration for the approach I have developed here.[62] But it is important to understand that the argument I develop about sharing cannot be encompassed within an analysis of government (or governmentality). Chatterjee's account focuses chiefly on the work of government in the postcolonial world, which in his account occurs via a kind of administrative power exercised over populations, often via the workings not of representative democracy ("civil society") but of what he calls "political society." While I share Chatterjee's interest in the government of "denizens," the fundamental object of my investigation here is not government, but the process through which people can achieve distributions, the way they can, through their presence, access what I call "shares." Such distributions may certainly come about as a result of the process of being governed (e.g., the cash-transfer programs I analyzed in *Give a Man a Fish*). But they may also be achieved in ways that have no such direct connection with government, or that are a kind of accidental byproduct of it—such as when rightless migrants to the city manage to benefit from public provisioning not intended for them (including urban infrastructure, as I have discussed above; see pp. 29–33). Here, the power of presence operates not via a claim on government, but by creating practical possibilities to "help oneself." If there is sharing here, it is not the deliberate allocation of resources by the developmental state but something more like demand sharing—in which, as Widlok has pointed out, among the most important forms of sharing is the practice of "refraining from inter-fering with someone who is about to take something."[63] This mode of gaining shares is not really captured in the idea of government as an administrative power exercised over a population, but I argue that it is an important part of how people gain shares in practice via presence.

Arendt

The essay closes with a quotation from Hannah Arendt, and I fear this may lead the reader to associate my stance more closely with hers than would be appropriate. I am drawn to the quotation because it beautifully expresses the way that a kind of involuntary living-in-one-another's-presence is both a necessary and a joyful part of human life. But I also wish to make clear that Arendt's concept of "plurality" gives what she calls "presence" a much narrower role than what I have in mind. She sees the significance of plural-ity chiefly in a kind of prepolitical recognition—the presence of others allows us to see ourselves through other eyes, in the process enabling a sense of reality. But her account grants "plurality" none of the larger political and social significance that I see in presence. For Arendt, real politics is found only in a specifically political community, understood in terms of a conven-tional idea of dialogue and deliberation in the public sphere. The "social" for her is precisely *not* political—a stance that led her to her now-notorious defense of school segregation in the US as a "social" rather than "political" matter.[64]

In contrast to Arendt, my whole point is that significant kinds of living together (including those that may yield certain kinds of social obligation) take form even where there is little or no political community in Arendt's sense—where people don't speak the same language, don't share a common history and culture, and do not come together via an act of will to debate their shared future. Instead, they are thrown together (see Liisa Malkki on "accidental communities of memory")[65] into something that does not resemble Arendt's polis, but that does have at least some of the key characteristics of "society," including the capacity to create social obligation.

Butler

In recent years, Judith Butler has given welcome attention to several issues that are related to the key arguments of my essay, including the ethical significance of precarity, vulnerability, and infrastructure.[66] She has also recently addressed the question of the way that ethical obligations may apply to people living in conditions of "unwilled adjacency," a theme with obvious overlaps with my own concerns. Of special interest, too (given my comments in the preceding reading note), is that she offers a useful critical rereading of Arendt's account that, in its emphasis on shared vulnerability, converges with some of the anthropological ways of thinking I have tried to develop here. Precarity, Butler writes, "is indissociable from that dimension of politics that addresses the organization and protection of bodily needs. Precarity exposes our sociality, the fragile and necessary dimensions of our interdependency."[67]

With all this, I am in broad sympathy, if not point-for-point agreement. But for the sake of clarity, I also wish to point out three key differences of emphasis in the two approaches. First, and most obviously, Butler's whole investigation involves asking what things like "precarity" or being "up against" others mean "for our ethical obligations."[68] The whole issue of obligation is turned into a question about "our" ethical obligation, with no attempt to understand social obligation in the anthropological sense (see the reading note on the social-anthropology tradition, above).[69]

Second, Butler's account of ethical obligations toward proximate or adjacent others relies not only on shared vulnerability (as in my account), but also on the fact that "there are others out there on whom my life depends."[70] This points to a conventional sort of mutuality based in reciprocal dependence, but it has nothing to say about the more challenging sort of obligation to share found in demand sharing, which requires us to consider all those *other* others "out there" on whom my life does *not* depend—but who are "here," and who may by virtue of that fact make claims to shares (e.g., the fellow passengers in the taxi, or the newly unemployed farm workers I pointed to in my critique of Ehrenreich).

Finally, a third difference of emphasis is that Butler seems interested in the power of physical proximity almost exclusively in a conventionally "political" context (in the form of "assembly," such as the demonstration, "the street," "occupy" movements). This seems to me to bypass the most important ways that such proximity actually makes itself felt, in favor of what Clive Barnett has recently termed a "romantic preference for performative models of assembly and demonstration and protest."[71] The result (an unfortunate one from my point of view) is to leave the everyday social relations of adjacency that I have argued are so central to the levying of many kinds of distributive claims simply outside the scope of a "political" analysis. ∎

Endnotes

Preface

1. Eileen Ng, "Singapore Sentences Drug Dealer to Death at Zoom Hearing," Associated Press, May 20, 2020, apnews.com/article/a8569980bbf1a511e9ed55db18e5bb34.

Introduction: Why Social Obligation? Why Now?

2. James Ferguson and Tania Li, "Beyond the 'Proper Job': Political-Economic Analysis after the Century of Labouring Man," PLAAS Working Paper 51, University of the Western Cape, Cape Town, April 2018.
3. The following four paragraphs borrow from Ferguson and Li, "Beyond the 'Proper Job,'" and should be regarded as jointly authored.
4. Guy Standing, *Beyond the New Paternalism: Basic Security as Equality* (New York: Verso, 2002), 7.
5. Michael Denning, "Wageless Life," *New Left Review* 66 (2010).
6. James Ferguson, *Give a Man a Fish: Reflections on the New Politics of Distribution* (Durham, NC: Duke University Press, 2015).
7. Ferguson, *Give a Man a Fish.*
8. Ferguson, *Give a Man a Fish*, 179–83.
9. Ferguson, *Give a Man a Fish*, 56.

Presence and Social Obligation: An Essay on the Share

10. Nikolas Rose, "The Death of the Social? Re-figuring the Territory of Government," *Economy and Society* 25, no. 3 (2006).
11. Bruno Latour, *Reassembling the Social: An Introduction to Actor-Network-Theory* (New York: Oxford University Press, 2005); cf. Michael Callon, "Some Elements of a Sociology of Translation: Domestication of the Scallops and the Fishermen of St Brieuc Bay," *Sociological Review* 32, no. 1_suppl (1984).
12. Tobias Rees, "Humanity/Plan; or, On the 'Stateless' Today (Also Being an Anthropology of Global Health)," *Cultural Anthropology* 29, no. 3 (2014), doi.org/10.14506/ca29.3.02.
13. On the actual motives of "humanitarian" volunteers (which turn out to be a good deal more complicated than is sometimes imagined), see Liisa H. Malkki, *The Need to Help: The Domestic*

Arts of International Humanitarianism (Durham, NC: Duke University Press, 2015).

14. For a lucid explanation of the anthropological distinction between gift and share, and a compelling argument against the analytical assimilation of sharing with reciprocal exchange, see Thomas Widlok, *Anthropology and the Economy of Sharing* (New York: Routledge, 2017), 1–29.

15. Some exceptions are discussed in the conclusion to *Give a Man a Fish*. The worldwide basic-income organization, the Basic Income Earth Network, subscribes (as its name suggests) to a planetary scope as a kind of ultimate ideal, but specific activist and legislative campaigns generally remain at the national level.

16. See Thomas Widlok, "Virtue," in *A Companion to Moral Anthropology*, ed. Didier Fassin (Hoboken, NJ: John Wiley, 2012).

17. Let me be clear that I do not imply by this any disrespect to the lively and learned discussions in political philosophy dealing with obligation and rights in the context of discussions of place and citizenship, which are both impressive and important—see, e.g., Paulina Ochoa Espejo, "Taking Place Seriously: Territorial Presence and the Rights of Immigrants," *Journal of Political Philosophy* 24, no. 1 (2016); Jeremy Waldron, "The Principle of Proximity" (Public Research Law Paper no. 11-08, New York University School of Law, January 2011); and, from a rather different perspective, Étienne Balibar, "Toward Co-Citizenship," in *Equaliberty: Political Essays*, trans. James Ingram (Durham, NC: Duke University Press, 2014). But instead of seeking to answer a normative, "ought" question ("How should liberal democracies treat non-citizens who are already physically present in their territory," as Ochoa Espejo puts it in "Taking Place Seriously," 67), I pursue the more anthropological approach of starting with a better understanding of the "is"—an understanding of how those lacking membership in fact manage to turn their presence into the ground for effective distributive claims.

18. Marcel Mauss, *The Gift: The Form and Reason for Exchange in Archaic Societies*, trans. W. E. Halls (1924; New York: W. W. Norton, 2000).

19. Here, I have been influenced by an extensive anthropological literature on sharing (see "Addendum: Some Theoretical Contrasts and Clarifications"), and especially by the work of

Thomas Widlok. See his extensive review of the literature on sharing in general, and on "demand sharing" in particular, in Widlok, *Anthropology and the Economy of Sharing*.

20. Nicolas Peterson, "Demand Sharing: Reciprocity and the Pressure for Generosity among Foragers," *American Anthropologist*, n.s., 95, no. 4 (1993).

21. See, e.g., for Zimbabwe, David Lan, *Guns and Rain: Guerrillas and Spirit Mediums in Zimbabwe* (Berkeley: University of California Press, 1985); Donald Moore, *Suffering for Territory: Race, Place, and Power in Zimbabwe* (Durham, NC: Duke University Press, 2005).

22. That the difference between southern African and US conceptions is not an absolute one is seen in the role that "shared suffering" can play in the American process of granting legal citizenship (for instance, when military service may, in some circumstances, help "naturalize" a foreigner into an American).

23. Patience Ntelamo Mususa, "There Used to Be Order: Life on the Copperbelt after the Privatisation of the Zambia Consolidated Copper Mines" (PhD diss., University of Cape Town, 2014), 133.

24. Ibid.

25. Widlok, *Anthropology and the Economy of Sharing*, 28.

26. The very fact that we so readily reduce presence-based distributive obligation to the "micro" level of society shows the link between obligation, distribution, and the *domestic*—as if obligation is fundamentally familial, and sharing rooted in the home (cf. Ferguson, *Give a Man a Fish*). This shows the importance both of distinguishing presence from belonging (being "here" vs. being "one of us"), and of attending to scale (if social belonging is routinely "scaled up" to nationality, then face-to-face presence too must be scaled up to a political status rooted in an expanded conception of being "here" and "among us").

27. Partha Chatterjee, *The Politics of the Governed: Reflections on Popular Politics in Most of the World* (New York: Columbia University Press, 1993).

28. Anne-Maria Makhulu, *Making Freedom: Apartheid, Squatter Politics, and the Struggle for Home* (Durham, NC: Duke University Press, 2015).

29. Compare Liisa Malkki on "accidental communities of memory," in "News and Culture: Transitory Phenomena and the

Fieldwork Tradition," in *Anthropological Locations: Boundaries and Grounds of a Field Science*, ed. Akhil Gupa and James Ferguson (Berkeley: University of California Press, 1997).

30. Didier Fassin, *Humanitarian Reason: A Moral History of the Present*, trans. Rachel Gomme (Berkeley: University of California Press, 2012).

31. Clive Barnett and David Land, "Geographies of Generosity: Beyond the 'Moral Turn,'" *Geoforum* 38, no. 6 (2007).

32. See "Addendum: Some Theoretical Contrasts and Clarifications" for a discussion of the genuinely obligatory nature of the social obligation to share.

33. Giorgio Agamben, *Homo Sacer: Sovereign Power and Bare Life*, trans. Daniel Heller-Roazen (Stanford, CA: Stanford University Press, 1998).

34. Gilbert K. Chesterton, *Heretics* (London: John Lane, 1905), 186. For a stimulating discussion of the political possibilities of the theological figure of the neighbor, see Slavoj Žižek, Eric L. Santner, and Kenneth Reinhard, *The Neighbor: Three Inquiries in Political Theology* (2005; Chicago: University of Chicago Press, 2013).

35. Antina von Schnitzler, *Democracy's Infrastructure: Techno-Politics and Protest after Apartheid* (Princeton, NJ: Princeton University Press, 2016).

36. Chatterjee, *Politics of the Governed*.

37. Jacob Doherty, "Life (and Limb) in the Fast-Lane: Disposable People as Infrastructure in Kampala's Boda Boda Industry," *Critical African Studies* 9, no. 2 (2017); "Capitalizing Community: Waste, Wealth, and (Im)material Labor in a Kampala Slum," *International Labor and Working-Class History* 95 (2019); "Filthy Flourishing: Para-Sites, Animal Infrastructure, and the Waste Frontier in Kampala." *Current Anthropology* 60, no. S20 (2019); "Maintenance Space: The Political Authority of Garbage in Kampala, Uganda," *Current Anthropology* 60, no. 1 (2019).

38. Gabrielle Hecht, "Residue," *Somatosphere*, January 8, 2018, somatosphere.net/2018/residue.html/; "Interscalar Vehicles for an African Anthropocene: On Waste, Temporality, and Violence," *Cultural Anthropology* 33, no. 1 (2108).

39. Mike Davis, *Planet of Slums* (New York: Verso, 2006); Robert D. Kaplan, "The Coming Anarchy," *The Atlantic*, February 1994.

40. See, e.g., "Emerging and Developing Economies Much More Optimistic than Rich Countries about the Future," Pew Research Center, October 9, 2014, www.pewglobal.org/2014/10/09/emerging-and-developing-economies-much-more-optimistic-than-rich-countries-about-the-future/.

41. Cf. James Ferguson, "Proletarian Politics Today: On the Perils and Possibilities of Historical Analogy," *Comparative Studies in Society and History* 61, no. 1 (2019).

42. This formulation may recall Asef Bayat's conception of an "art of presence" that is a key part of what he terms "life as politics." But while Bayat simply fuses "life" and "politics," rendering presence itself already political, I emphasize the work of critical reframing and social recognition that is necessary before the brute fact of presence can present itself as political. In my terms, this involves bringing the figuration of being "here among us" into relation with that of being "one of us." See *Life as Politics: How Ordinary People Change the Middle East* (Stanford, CA: Stanford University Press, 2013).

43. Barnett and Land, "Geographies of Generosity."

44. See "Addendum: Some Theoretical Contrasts and Clarifications" on the idea of "rendering" presence; cf. Jacques Derrida, *Of Grammatology*, trans. Gayatri Chakravorty Spivak (Baltimore: Johns Hopkins University Press, 1974); Matthew Engelke, *A Problem of Presence: Beyond Scripture in an African Church* (Berkeley: University of California Press, 2007).

45. "The Global Philosopher: Should Borders Be Abolished?," *BBC Magazine*, March 22, 2016, www.bbc.com/news/magazine-35834178.

46. There is of course a rich theoretical literature on social and political recognition. See, e.g., Paul Ricoeur, *The Course of Recognition*, trans. David Pellauer (Cambridge, MA: Harvard University Press, 2005); Nancy Fraser and Axel Honneth, *Redistribution or Recognition: A Political-Philosophical Exchange* (New York: Verso, 2003); and (in an African context) Harri Englund and Francis Nyamnjoh, eds., *Rights and the Politics of Recognition in Africa* (London: Zed, 2004).

47. See the insightful discussion in Ochoa Espejo, "Taking Place Seriously."

48. Seth Holmes, *Fresh Fruit, Broken Bodies: Migrant Farmworkers in the United States* (Berkeley: University of California Press, 2013).

49. Barbara Ehrenreich, "The Selfish Side of Gratitude," *New York Times*, January 3, 2016, www.nytimes.com/2016/01/03/opinion/sunday/the-selfish-side-of-gratitude.html.

50. I am not able here to deal with the important and interesting issue of the ways that electronically mediated forms of sociality ("social media") may (or may not) involve "presence" in my sense. What seems clear to me is that (1) the question is a complex one, without any simple answer, and (2) it really needs to be addressed by someone who has a much better practical and theoretical understanding of contemporary social media than I do. I will note just that the key issue seems to me the way that presence, in my sense, always enables a sociality that goes beyond the exchange of information to render the participants in some sense genuinely exposed and vulnerable (in the way that a face-to-face insult may earn the insulter a quick punch in the nose). One could no doubt identify analogues of such exposure and vulnerability in some forms of electronic sociality, but the extent to which such analogs really function in the ways that I have described for bodily presence is no doubt a matter for further thought and research. For a stimulating discussion, see Widlok, *Anthropology and the Economy of Sharing*, 163–96.

51. Hannah Arendt, *The Human Condition* (1958; repr., Chicago: University of Chicago Press, 1998), 244.

Addendum: Some Theoretical Contrasts and Clarifications

52. *Merriam-Webster*, s.v. "obligatory (*adj.*)," accessed August 1, 2020, www.merriam-webster.com/dictionary/obligatory.

53. Vocabulary.com, s.v. "obligatory (*adj.*)," accessed August 1, 2020, www.vocabulary.com/dictionary/obligatory.

54. Elizabeth Colson, *Tradition and Contract: The Problem of Order* (Chicago: Aldine, 1974), 47–49.

55. A similar dynamic can be observed in the coercive pressures often applied by kin and others for sharing by absent or returning migrant workers. I have explored this in detail in one southern African case. See James Ferguson, *Expectations of Modernity: Myths and Meanings of Urban Life on the Zambian Copperbelt* (Berkeley: University of California Press, 1999).

56. Colson, *Tradition and Contract*, 37. I am grateful to Kerem Ussakli for bringing this quotation to my attention.

57. Émile Durkheim, *The Elementary Forms of Religious Life*, trans. Karen E. Fields (1912; New York: Free Press, 1995).

58. See, e.g., Latour, *Reassembling the Social.*

59. For the scallops case, see Callon, "Some Elements of a Sociology of Translation."

60. See, especially, Derrida, *Of Grammatology.*

61. See Engelke, *A Problem of Presence.*

62. See, especially, Chatterjee, *The Politics of the Governed.*

63. Widlok, *Anthropology and the Economy of Sharing*, 28.

64. See Kathryn T. Gines, *Hannah Arendt and the Negro Question* (Bloomington: Indiana University Press, 2014).

65. Malkki, "News and Culture."

66. See Judith Butler, *Precarious Life: The Powers of Mourning and Violence* (New York: Verso, 2004), and *Notes toward a Performative Theory of Assembly* (Cambridge, MA: Harvard University Press, 2015).

67. Butler, *Notes toward a Performative Theory of Assembly*, 119.

68. Ibid., 99.

69. I note in passing (and all too briefly) that the same seems to me true of other figurations of social obligation that one encounters in contemporary "theory" (such as "hospitality" or "care")—here too I am sympathetic with the endeavor, but find that the focus of the literature on drawing normative conclusions ("our ethical obligations") too often limits its ability to grasp the issues that anthropologists may find the most important ones, such as when and why duties of hospitality, care, or any other sort are in fact understood to be (or not to be) obligatory in a specific social context.

70. Butler, *Precarious Life*, xii.

71. Clive Barnett, "Geography and the Priority of Injustice," *Annals of the American Association of Geographers* 108, no. 2 (2018): 325.

Also available from Prickly Paradigm Press:

continued

continued